Visit and Learn

Devils Tower

by Roxanne Troup

FOCUS
READERS.

BEACON

www.focusreaders.com

Copyright © 2024 by Focus Readers®, Lake Elmo, MN 55042. All rights reserved. No part of this book may be reproduced or utilized in any form or by any means without written permission from the publisher.

Focus Readers is distributed by North Star Editions:
sales@northstareditions.com | 888-417-0195

Produced for Focus Readers by Red Line Editorial.

Photographs ©: Shutterstock Images, cover, 1, 4, 7, 8, 11, 13, 16, 19, 21, 22, 26, 29; John C.H. Grabill/ Library of Congress, 14–15; iStockphoto, 25

Library of Congress Cataloging-in-Publication Data
Names: Troup, Roxanne, author.
Title: Devils Tower / Roxanne Troup.
Description: Lake Elmo, MN: Focus Readers, [2024] | Includes
  bibliographical references and index. | Audience: Grades 2-3
Identifiers: LCCN 2022058464 (print) | LCCN 2022058465 (ebook) | ISBN
  9781637396162 (hardcover) | ISBN 9781637396735 (paperback) | ISBN
  9781637397831 (ebook pdf) | ISBN 9781637397305 (hosted ebook)
Subjects: LCSH: Devils Tower National Monument (Wyo.)--Juvenile literature.
Classification: LCC F767.D47 T76 2024 (print) | LCC F767.D47 (ebook) |
  DDC 978.7/13--dc23/eng/20221214
LC record available at https://lccn.loc.gov/2022058464
LC ebook record available at https://lccn.loc.gov/2022058465

Printed in the United States of America
Mankato, MN
082023

About the Author

Author of more than a dozen books for kids, Roxanne Troup writes engaging nonfiction for all ages. She lives in the mountains of Colorado and loves visiting state and national parks to hike with her family. She also enjoys visiting schools to promote literacy and teach about writing.

Table of Contents

Chapter 1

A Natural Wonder

A hiker sees a huge stone tower up ahead. It rises high above the plains. From a distance, it looks like a giant tree stump. But it is actually a **butte**. It is called Devils Tower.

Devils Tower looms high above the surrounding countryside.

Buttes form in dry, desert-like conditions. They have steep sides and flat tops. Buttes are common in places such as the American West.

Devils Tower is in northeast Wyoming. This area is part of the Black Hills region. The butte stands 1,267 feet (386 m) high. Its base

Did You Know?

Devils Tower is popular with rock climbers. For most people, it takes about five hours to reach the top.

 Climbers can use several different routes to reach the top of Devils Tower.

is nearly 1 mile (1.6 km) around.

But its top is only the size of a

football field.

Chapter 2

Out of the Earth

No one knows exactly how Devils Tower formed. But scientists do know it is made of **igneous rock**. This type of rock is very hard. It forms when **magma** cools. As magma cools, it begins to crack.

 Compared to other types of rock, igneous rock is very hard.

Columns of rock form as a result. Each column has five or six sides.

Scientists think Devils Tower was once covered with **sedimentary rock**. This type of rock forms from pressed layers of mud and pebbles. Over time, this soft rock erodes. As it wears away, harder rock under the surface begins to show.

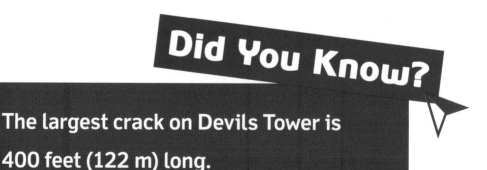

Did You Know?

The largest crack on Devils Tower is 400 feet (122 m) long.

 Sedimentary rock is made of many layers that build up over millions of years.

Some scientists believe Devils Tower formed deep underground. Others think it is part of an old volcano.

However it formed, Devils Tower has inspired many stories. People have talked about it for thousands of years. The Kiowa people say the rock grew out of the ground like a giant tree. It saved seven girls from a bear attack.

The Cheyenne people say the rock protected their warriors from a giant bear. The bear jumped for the men. But it couldn't reach them. Its powerful claws scratched the rock and formed the columns.

 Native dancers wear traditional clothing during an event in Wyoming.

The Lakota people call the rock *Mato Tipila*, or Bear Lodge. Other Native Nations tell similar stories about the rock. Each of these Nations considers it a **sacred** place.

Different Names

Devils Tower has not always been called by that name. Before 1875, it was known as Bear Lodge or Bear Tipi. However, a US soldier renamed it Devils Tower. He may have misunderstood the rock's Lakota name. Or he may have ignored it. No one knows. Either way, the new name stuck.

Today, several Native Nations are working to have the name changed. Each of these Nations has its own connection to the rock. All agree it's not an evil place, like the current name suggests.

A picture from 1888 refers to the rock as both Devils Tower and Bear Lodge.

No. 888. "DEVIL'S TOW
Devil's Tower or Bear Lodge,
of the Indians,) as seen from
Located near the Belle Fourc
Wyoming.
(Photo. and copyright by O.

15

Chapter 3

Protected for All

In 1906, Devils Tower became the first national **monument** in the United States. President Theodore Roosevelt helped make it happen. He loved the outdoors. He wanted others to be able to enjoy it, too.

 Theodore Roosevelt visited many wilderness areas while he was president.

So, he placed the area around Devils Tower in a reserve. Anyone can visit. No one can build, hunt, or farm on the land.

Devils Tower is home to many animals. Deer, turkey, and porcupines roam the area. So do mink, bats, and muskrats. Mountain lions, bald eagles, and hawks also hunt nearby.

Black-tailed prairie dogs live at the tower's base. Prairie dogs live in large groups. They build

 A deer walks through a field near Devils Tower.

underground homes in the soft soil. However, their tunnels can be dangerous to cattle. So, farmers often try to remove them. As a result, the black-tailed prairie dog has become a threatened **species**.

But at Devils Tower, the animals are protected.

Falcons make their nests in the tower's cracks. Nesting falcons may dive at climbers who come too close. Or they may leave their nests if people come near. The baby birds can die as a result. So, every year,

Did You Know?

Prairie dogs are a type of ground squirrel. Their yips sound like a dog's bark. That's how they got their name.

> A prairie dog peeks out of its tunnel to watch for predators.

park rangers close sections of the tower. That helps protect climbers and falcon nests. Thanks in part to this work, these falcons are no longer **endangered**.

Chapter 4

Visiting Devils Tower

People from all over the world visit Devils Tower. Some people come to climb. Others come to look at nature. Many visitors hike. They also watch birds. At night, they gaze at stars.

 The area around Devils Tower includes forest, prairie, and river habitats.

Visitors can attend programs about the history of Devils Tower. They can also go on tours led by rangers.

Weather changes quickly at Devils Tower. Visitors need to be prepared, especially in the spring or fall. Days may start out cold. But they warm up fast. High winds and

Did You Know?

In 2021, more than 500,000 people visited Devils Tower.

 Devils Tower offers several different hiking trails. The Tower Trail is the most popular.

storms are common in summer. So, climbers must be very careful.

In June, people from many Native Nations visit the tower. They come to honor their history. They also celebrate their **culture**.

 Prayer cloths are tied to a tree near Devils Tower.

The National Park Service asks visitors to respect these events. They suggest not climbing the tower in June. They also tell visitors to never remove prayer cloths.

These cloths are an important part of religious ceremonies.

Park rangers help visitors stay safe. They remind visitors not to feed or touch animals. Rangers also ask people to leave no trace. That means visitors should pick up their trash. Also, they should not remove plants or rocks. Instead, they should leave the park exactly as they found it. That way, new visitors can enjoy Devils Tower for years to come.

FOCUS ON
Devils Tower

Write your answers on a separate piece of paper.

1. Write a paragraph explaining the main ideas of Chapter 2.

2. Would you climb Devils Tower? Why or why not?

3. What other name is Devils Tower known by?
   - **A.** Falcon Nest
   - **B.** Giant Stump
   - **C.** Bear Lodge

4. Why do park rangers close some climbing routes on Devils Tower?
   - **A.** to protect baby falcons
   - **B.** to help prairie dogs stay healthy
   - **C.** to keep the tower from eroding

5. What does **erodes** mean in this book?

*Over time, this soft rock **erodes**. As it wears away, harder rock under the surface begins to show.*

    A. becomes harder and sharper
    B. wears away slowly over time
    C. turns into a new material

6. What does **reserve** mean in this book?

*So, he placed the area around Devils Tower in a **reserve**. Anyone can visit. No one can build, hunt, or farm on the land.*

    A. land that is dangerous to visit
    B. land that is saved and protected
    C. land that only animals can use

Answer key on page 32.

Glossary

butte
A landform with steep sides and a flat top.

culture
The way a group of people live; their customs, beliefs, and laws.

endangered
In danger of dying out.

igneous rock
A type of rock that forms when magma cools.

magma
Hot, melted rock under Earth's surface.

monument
A building or structure that is of historical interest or importance.

sacred
Having spiritual or religious meaning.

sedimentary rock
A type of rock that forms when particles settle to the bottom of a lake or river, build up in layers, and turn to stone.

species
A group of animals or plants that are alike and can breed with one another.

To Learn More

BOOKS

Bird, F. A. *Sioux*. Minneapolis: Abdo Publishing, 2022.

Murray, Laura K. *Wyoming*. Minneapolis: Abdo Publishing, 2023.

Payne, Stefanie. *The National Parks: Discover All 62 National Parks of the United States*. New York: DK Publishing, 2020.

NOTE TO EDUCATORS

Visit **www.focusreaders.com** to find lesson plans, activities, links, and other resources related to this title.

Index

B

Black Hills, 6

buttes, 5–7

C

Cheyenne people, 12

climbing, 6, 20–21, 23, 25–26

F

falcons, 20–21

I

igneous rock, 9

K

Kiowa people, 12

L

Lakota people, 13, 14

M

magma, 9

N

names, 14

Native Nations, 12–13, 14, 25

P

prairie dogs, 18–20

prayer cloths, 26–27

R

rangers, 21, 24, 27

Roosevelt, Theodore, 17

S

sedimentary rock, 10

W

weather, 24–25

Answer Key: 1. Answers will vary; 2. Answers will vary; 3. C; 4. A; 5. B; 6. B